Pat Borthwick

Admiral FitzRoy's Barometer

Templar Poetry

First Published 2008 by Templar Poetry
Templar Poetry is an imprint of Delamide & Bell

Fenelon House,
Kingsbridge Terrace
58 Dale Road, Matlock, Derbyshire
DE4 3NB

www.templarpoetry.co.uk

ISBN 978-1-906285-20-3

A CIP catalogue record of this book is available from the British Library.

Typeset by Pliny
Graphics by Paloma Violet
Printed and bound in Turkey

For Tim, my son, and the bright light of friends

From this the poem springs: that we live in a place
That is not our own and, much more, not ourselves.

Wallace Stevens

Acknowledgements

'Guest Room', 2nd Prize Manchester Cathedral Poems on Spirituality 2006:
'Shaft', The McLelland Award 2007, HC: 'Snake', 2nd Prize Anglo-Canadian
Petra Kenney2005 and 'Swim' (Mudfog 2005): 'Past Twelve O'clock', 1st Prize
Scintilla 2005: 'Lost Spoon', chosen by Julia Darling as the Poem of the Month
for the Diamond Twig website 2006: 'The Tale', 2nd Prize Scintilla 2006 (part of
a longer sequence): 'One of My Fathers', Myslexia R-up 2005: 'Chair', Ink on
Paper (Mudfog/mima): 'Passing On the Tickle', 1st Prize Silver Wyvern, Poetry
on the Lake, Italy 2006 and 'Wave' (Templar 2007): 'It's Only', 2nd Prize,
Frogmore 2005: 'Whale Watch', Leaf Books 2006: 'The Song the Letters Sing',
(Seam 12, 2007): 'Becoming Woman', Anglo-Canadian Petra Kenney HC 2008:
'Apple Pie', 1st Prize Second Light 2008; 'Katya', 1st prize Amnesty
International Human Rights 2005 and 'Swim' (Mudfog 2005) and 'Wave'
(Templar 2007): 'Admiral FitRoy's Barometer', Feeling the Pressure (British
Council Anthology 2008): 'And Last of All', (Orbis 2007): 'Grass', 2nd Prize
Torriano Open 2006 and 'Wave'(Templar 2007): 'The First Moose to Try It',
Nottingham Open R-up 2005: 'Wheelbarrow', Poetry Nottingham 2006: 'The
Old Observatory', 3rd Prize Iota 2007: 'Feeding the Bi-Valve', Winner of Blue
Nose Poet of the Year: 'The Widower's Button', 1st Prize Envoi 2008: 'In The
Consulting Room', 2nd Prize Anglo-Canadian Petra Kenney 2006 and 'Wave'
(Templar 2007): 'Visiting Father', 'Wave' (Templar 2007): 'In Praise of the
Oologist's Art', 1st Prize Scintilla 2007 and 'Wave' (Templar 2007): 'The Wash',
Troubadour R-up 2008.

My special thanks go to the Arvon Foundation, Roger Garfitt at Madingley, Ty
Newydd, The Poetry School, The Poetry Business, Aldeburgh, Beverley and
StAnza Festivals and Chris North at Almassera, Spain who have provided
inspiring programmes of courses, workshops and speakers: to Alex McMillen at
Templar Poetry:

and to the generous and much appreciated encouragement from poet friends.

Contents

Guest Room	1
Shaft	2
At least 51 Ways of Contemplating a Hole	4
Snake	5
Tavistock Square	7
Past Twelve O'clock	9
At This Moment	11
En Plein Air	13
Whale Watch	15
Lost Spoon	16
My Neighbour's Myna	17
The Tale	19
Sometimes a Camel	21
One of my Fathers	22
Chair	24
Passing On the Tickle	25
First Words	27
The Song the Letters Sing	28
Becoming Woman	29
Last Day of the Holiday	31
Apple Pie	32
Admiral FitzRoy's Barometer	34
Katya	35
Visiting Father....	37
Stone	38
Interlude	39
Seeking a Bittern	42
In Praise of the Oologist's Art	44
Grass	46
Grasshopper	48
Forecast	49
The First Moose To Try It	50
The Old Observatory	52
Feeding the Bi-valve	53
The Widower's Button	54
In The Consulting Room	56

In Praise of Grey   58
Wholly   59
The Wash   61
A Very Private Conversation   62

Guest Room

Some tiny creature
right outside my window,
woke me.

It might have been
the warm-up act, a solo,
centre-stage in the bracken
or hedge bottom
but it was highly metabolic
and pitched above angels.

Imagine a chandelier in Versailles
shaken with the speed of light:
a canteen of cutlery
falling from a plane's baggage hold –
then you're close.

And imagine,
over the tick of my alarm,
the muscle of a little fragrant heart.

Shaft

Even before they sank this well
to give the spring its echo,
water giggled and gurgled underground

through watery lips, as if divining us.
It's a brutal business hacking with picks,
shovelling earth and stone.

A man with a hammer, held by rope,
shutters the shaft with good green oak.
When suddenly it's there.

He stares at one wet eye
staring back at him,
amazed by the light's flash flood.

It'll take bricks and mortar,
a carpenter and smith,
before the first pail is lowered

and a priest stand with an open book
first looking down, then up,
his raised hand blessing rain.

Soprano and bass; water is its own choir.
Hymns sing every valley.
There's plainsong in the cattle-troughs,

psalters in dewponds and lakes.
Something fancier over waterfalls.
Here, in the bottom of this well

is wolf and mountain, thunder and fire.
Each colour they've lived. Listen.
There is not one sound they cannot sing.

And never the same note twice.
In every bucket drawn up: a gallon of sky,
a galaxy of stars. Not a drop must be spilt.

At Least 51 Ways of Contemplating a Hole

Head	Zero	Ring	Yawn	Mole	Bore	Vent	Dark
Void	Cave	Dint	Port	Gone	Peep	Oval	Duck
Only	Open	None			Love	Lost	Moon
Left	Disc	Null	Hope		Gape	Lone	Cake
Sole	Tube	Blow			Miss	Sans	Dent
Iris	Bole	Bolt	Worm	Gulf	Coal	Oust	Disk
Pore	Flue	Nail	Loop	Solo	Deep	Hoop	Mine

Snake

Just a glimpse of my bare heel or toe,
the slightest movement of my sheet
would alert a knotted writhe of snakes
lurking in the cave beneath my bed.
Heavy with poison,
they'd be slung between the springs,
coiled around the metal frame
or simply thick in number, camouflaged
among the carpet pattern's twists and turns,
their bifurcated tongues
wavering between needle-teeth and fangs.
They'd strike at the sight of a pale insole
or ankle, better still, a plumper calf.
When my night screams
brought the man married to my mother
he'd cover my mouth
then reticulate his other hand
between my grooves and hollows.
His tongue, strung with saliva,
would engulf and swallow me
as he delivered his shot of venom.

After the ringing in my ears had stopped
I'd fly into a treetop nest and sway there.
Coach whip, copper head, bull snake,
python, diamond back, smooth snake,
cobra, mamba, sidewinder, hoop snake,
house snake, ophidia, serpentes, my mantra.

I've gained their confidence. *Come up,*
I'll say, and then, in their jewelled tuxedos,
watch them stretch across my pillows,
slither below my duvet. Each time
I am surprised how warm they are,
how sleek their polished scales.
Who'd have guessed I'd have them
eating from my hand? I can
even stroke and squeeze them
while they nudge for more, their dewy eye
not fooling me. I've spent years
learning to unhook my jaw, perfect
the toxicity of my digestive juices
so not a single drop's superfluous.
See how much breath I hold
in this single, elongated lung.
See how I've sloughed my childskin.

Tavistock Square

July 2005

It wasn't when the jazz band underneath
the cherry tree had packed away their notes

nor when Punch and Judy bowed
then disappeared behind stripy curtains

and it wasn't as one by one
hungry buggies were wheeled off past Gandhi

nor when people on the benches near Virginia
and Dickens (in Memory of Tom and Nan, Arthur

and George) helped each other up, See you
tomorrow? the fat pigeons flapping off (coo-ooee)

to settle on metal heads, triumphant arms,
nor when a sudden blazered man

pedalled through on a penny-farthing,
or the café shuttered up and joggers left,

nor when one by one (including an old priest)
everybody picked themselves from the grass,

that,   just before the wind rolled green leaves
towards the iron gates and a red bus beyond,

you could hear the park's animals breathing,
and their occasional dreaming:

distant little yelps and shuffles as if
they knew tomorrow would hold no sun,

the soft sound of twitching paws
as if they had already started to run.

Past Twelve O'clock

Through a radio's crackle,
Big Ben, slower than usual,
booms out its chimes.
Twelve o'clock.
It puts its hands together
over a downcast face.

We assemble out on the gravel.

Something has made the sun angry.
Insects unbusy themselves.
Birds wing to the nearest chimney
or branch. Even the flighty clouds
hold their shape as they brake to a halt.

From behind droop-head roses
a child, who knows no reason
for silence, protests. Which is,
I suppose, what we're all here for
in this summoning of bells.

Buoys hard on their chains
have bells that taunt with their echo.
They are more doleful than London's
more vague. Some bells are sweet,
like cathedral bells that ripple
round the Close or mark the Millennia
by ringing in a great choir of bells,
a community of bells, their gaiety
appealing to every kissable inch of our land.

And I was a bell tolling in my mother.
My mother, a bell, is tolling in me.
And I was a bell calling men from the fields.
And I was a silent bell on the end of a phone.
And once I mistook myself for a prayer bell
and ran as fast as I could helter-skelter akimbo.
Only just in time.   But I sang when hung
from the neck of a mountain goat or a cow.
Life then was a grassy tide with no time for time.

They say that the Earth is a bell
forged in a roar of light,
sent spinning through stars to here.
Imagine its knell filling still and silent spaces.
Then a dumb tongue.

En Plein Air

The pond is full to the brim of itself
and why shouldn't it be
seeing how the willow
has stripped naked to bathe there
among boat-shaped leaves.

Today, in sparkling gloves,
multi-fingered frost
ushers Autumn into Winter
while spiders' threads
snatch and weave the sun
as if to hold its pale warmth forever.

To attempt a permanence
where would the painter
place his first brushfull on the canvas?
Which first note would a composer pen
and for what instrument?

Listen,
    a robin shakes out his triplets,
      the crow, his dark vibrato.
          Another bird I cannot name
            snips the day into little pieces.

A coot runs on water softly splattering the silences between them.

Open faced,
the pond absorbs this flow,
but below its taut surface,
in a firmament of mud,
there is a rush of slow movement,
things not quite ready
to rise up through it and call,
Look, *we're here.*

We've named that Spring
although one day
it might not recognise its name.
O O O o o will sing the pond.

Whale Watch

A change of air you said
as if you'd just been reading
some yellowed fall-apart Home Medical.
I never understood how you thought
being far away might bring us home.

Our frothy wake fans towards the land,
the cape, bluing into distance.
With only a slap of wave, the diesel's throb,
our binoculars search empty horizons.

Later that night
the Atlantic bursts through our door.
Tail flukes slap on the ceiling.
You don't stir. Your side of the bed stays dry.
When you wake, you won't see wrack
hung from one half of the lightbulb,
a tern's forked feather
afloat on my empty pillow.

Lost Spoon

My body is like a lost spoon. Somewhere
at the back of the cutlery drawer
it has managed to lose itself in the clutter.
Is causing trouble again.
I can hear it cavorting with knives,
clattering against their blades.
Sweet-hearting them. One of their bone
or mother-of-pearl handles
bunts a comforting note in its bowl.
Now it's twanging the whisk,
weaving in and out of the egg-slice,
elbowing corncob holders. Such a flirt.
It's chattering up their knobbles.
Oh no, not the tin opener!
It's riding the wheels round and round
like being on that playground thing
next to the slide and the swings
I can see through my end ward window,
pushing along on one elegant silver limb.
And why not? We both know it's all bluff.
Let it have fun, practise being something
that can't be packed in a box.
Engraved with my copperplate name
it was there when I was christened
and has circled beside me since.
Soon enough it'll be asked
to stick out its tongue and say *Ah*
then filled with a measured dose
of something surprisingly weighty.
One day I'll bid it be still and it will -
perhaps something surprisingly sweet.

My Neighbour's Myna

No, of course I didn't mind.
He was marvellous company.

No, he was never a shriek of trouble.
I didn't even have to use the blanket.

But I was surprised when you rang,
told me you'd be away another month.

No, Harry and I got on together fine
chattering away till bedtime.

He's got the most beautiful eyes, hasn't he?
No wonder he liked being opposite the mirror,

the one above my fireplace, the one
I saw your car eventually come back in.

I'm amazed how quickly he picked things up,
the kettle's whistle, spitting logs, the top stair.

Oh, and that *fuckfuckfuck* must have come
from when I put the phone down on your call.

I'm afraid you'd ruffled my feathers.
People assume that because I'm on my own

I have no life to speak of. Well, * * * you.
He seems to like that sound the most you know.

Perhaps you could pretend he's saying,
Look, look. Rook! He's just as black. No, blacker.

You'll never guess what else he tried to do.
Has he ever had a go at that with you?

The Tale

There's something of amber
something magical
the way formaldehyde stops time.

In room 71 at the RCS
shelves of bottles and sealed flasks
stand labelled with the timeless strange.

Take Giant Bradley's hand
lopped off at his grave
or the foetus with two heads

both flatly staring back into the past.
Among hirsute and double genitalia,
elbows filled with grinning teeth,

is a dome-shaped jar
containing half a floating skull.
It's been cleaved in two

to reveal the brain's pale labyrinth,
with a black running stitch, exiting past
incus and drum to this shellscaped auricle.

One hopes that nose lost its sense of smell
and perhaps the single eye is dreaming
but turn the jar to see the outer ear

brimful with Dermaptera Forficulidae
(or so the label states), ear creatures,
with forceps as abdominal appendages,

all clamouring to join
a dark convoluted queue that reaches to
Man's CD-ROM and hard drive. It's a fact

that earwigs can't crawl backwards.
They emit foul stench and, with mandibles
as strong as steel, bore and chew

to lace the brain with madness while it sleeps.
As if Man can't manage that for himself
having such inferior wisdom to an earwig.

Sometimes a Camel

What can be seen through a window
that can't be seen anywhere,
in a fire perhaps, or wallpaper,
the shadow a camel casts across sand?
Or from this hotel bed where the ceiling's a screen.

There's a flicker in greys as the breeze outside
moves droops of wisteria across the frame then,
scattered, blown everywhere,
tiny human beings like broadcast seed,
none of them knowing where they'll fall to Earth.

Look, here come giraffes and polar bears,
a swarm of bees, fish whose sunlit scales
fill my room with rainbows.
I saw them earlier from the sofa in the lounge
swimming through flames in the hearth,
diving below coral, darting around an anchor
whose fluke reached through the grate
and into bedrock.
Who knows how close that fluke comes
to piercing the world's molten heart?

I can hear tethered camels complaining,
shifting their feet in the dunes as heat pours up
but now it's ice-cream time and adverts.

Tissue-wrapped soaps on the bathroom sill.
I'll take an early shower, wear the cap provided,
the one I'll descend the ladder to the moon in.
Even there
you'll still be ahead and following.

One of my Fathers

You're flat on the deck,
all the different shapes of you
stretched and gleaming
in the chrome bars round your bed.

I'm in a ringside seat but don't know why
except someone rang and said I'd miss it
if I didn't get here. I hear myself
punch out lies below flicking numbers

like: *every tomato in your greenhouse*
won Best of Show
like*: we're booked to fly on Concorde on Friday*
like*: you're grandmother sends her love*

Dad.   There, I've said it
and don't know how,
or why I'm holding your hand
while making up another lie

about donkeys trotting up a beach.
Neddy says *Ee-aw,* then nods.
You've not opened your eyes.
I tried to be asleep.

I would never have heard more
than the jingle of their headband bells
before your giant's hand
crept between my sheets.

A nurse asks if I'd sponge your lips?
But now I need both my hands
to pin down your one, until
another of my fathers comes along.

And perhaps I'll never work out why
I move in close, then quietly lean across
tolandthatlastfirstlastkiss with such speed
I can't be sure it counts. Or if I did.

Chair

A broken chair
leant against the allotment shed
casts its own row of shadows.

A widow will read them
in a different way to the child
who will see a line of animals,
waves rolling across the bay,
the gentle slopes of Grandad's sheets
before he left that Wednesday night
to visit somebody whose name,
always whispered,
sounded as if it started with a J –
like jelly and Grandad's geraniums.

There are times even a child knows
that some questions
must remain inside their head.

The plot grows thicker than a jungle.
There will be a season
when a broken chair,
propped against the leaning shed,
takes root, comes into leaf. Possibly
a flower or two.

Passing On the Tickle

Lie flat as sky, sleeves rolled to the elbow
so that, arms outstretched, your hands

hinge through the grassy overhang
to where water runs in shadows

and hollow reeds set notes free.
All possibilities are in this place.

It's here the speckled trout waits
gleaming in war-flecked armour.

For now, he's made himself invisible.
But you saw his flash of leap and catch,

his muddy swirl and dash.
And you know he faces upstream

breathing in, breathing out. And close —
his contemplation, the next plump fly

or next, the deliciousness of this one
snatched from heaven's bright mouth.

You were taught to watercreep your fingers
towards where he wafts his fins.

Are you closer to pectoral or pelvic,
the narrowing of sword to tail?

A clash of artistry. His argent muscle
tightens to attention as you make touch.

D-rum, d-rum, d-rumdiddy d-rum. He feels
your drowning beat. *D-rumdiddy d-rum.* Hook

two fingers in his closing gill and he's in air.
Your father, grandfather, his father, his,

throng the grassy bank, caps doffed.
Well done lad, well done. You watch

their hungry plates and cutlery
zig-zag to the bottom of the stream.

You are about to break your family line,
return him to his water. *D-rumdiddy d-rum.*

First Words

My daughter, in her third year,
finger-counting our Friesians
as they amble through the pasture,
and still no words.

That night, her first eclipse,
the Moon turned red,
its nearby stars
as pink as her quiet tongue.
Then, holding her
between rose-patterned curtains,
it was as if a star
had flitted through the glass
into her mouth
and, as she pointed to the Moon,
sounds poured from her
as though the whole Milky Way
had run down her throat.

And then,
that same night it seemed,
she learnt to speak
the names of constellations, even
what the planets that can't be seen
are called.

The Song the Letters Sing

A pple-mbulance-nt

B all-roken-at

C at-rashed-up

D og-river-ish

E ye-xamine-gg

F rog-atal-ish

G ate-rave-oat

H ospital-ome-at

I nk-nquest-vy

J ackknife-elly-am

K ite-erbstone-ey

L eaf-awyer-orry

M anslaughter-onkey-at

N ightmare-est-ut

O range-rphan-ctopus

P ig-ram-ronounced

Q ueen-uestions-uilt

R ecurrent-ed-oad

S un-ustain-ong

T ree-rial-ie

U mbrella-tmost-p

V iolin-iolent-an

W indmill-reckage-eb

X -ray-fo-ylophone

Y acht-esterday-ellow

Z ebra-ip-ombi

Becoming Woman

A sudden bear
comes at me upright,
all gravity, acceleration,
her spread-eagled claws
crusty with blood,
razored shreds of fish
swiped from the rapids.
I have to move
and the sky moves with me.
Black trees hurtle upwards
and I am held in their branches
looking down. Everything
is happening too fast, a river
bursting its banks.

She is on all fours now, as small
as the bear from my toy zoo.
I want to reach down
move her across the half-moon rug
past the crocodile on the border.
I need my mother to bring warm milk,
her hands, like ladles, to scoop me up.

But the flood is rising
and it's a hungry bear circling below.
Her wild muzzle leans into the air.
She mauls the space I've vanished from.
I can see her thick grey tongue,
her cavernous red-ridged throat.
There's a scent of fish,

things burrowing, scrambling,
plants pushing and unrolling.
My eyes shine like steel moons.

Roaring as I drop,
I ram my claws into her belly. Blood
flows through my nightie
and my mother is sitting on the bed.
I'm in the hoop of her arms.
Cotton wool and gauze.
A full moon leaning across
to greet me.

Last Day of the Holiday

The mail plane
ploughs through high blue
towards the mainland
with the letter I wrote yesterday,
stowed in its hold.

On Shell Beach
waves follow the quiet light
as it drains below the horizon.

Tomorrow, or the day after,
I will be that woman
who sits by a kettle
in an English home,
waiting for the postman
to come through her gate
and bring news
of who she once was

and how it is possible
to be her again.

Apple Pie

Blades peel hand-sized green apples.
Mother. Daughter. The routine of Sunday
overflushed with my first kiss.

Twin spirals work down to the countertop,
a silence sharp as lipstick red. Then
to your even sharper question, I answer truth,

name the film we saw and my new friend.
Dicing cold lard, you accuse me of lies.
I detail the plot. Again, you insist I lie.

Once you told me I'd get pregnant
if I talked to a boy on the phone,
that boys only wanted one thing

and that was never love. Scales clank
as you stack their honest weights
and flour-clouds thunder upwards.

Truth. Lie.   Truth. Lie.
Our words balance against each other's
then roll away, sticky as dough balls.

You have the rolling pin, work pastry
over the white ceramic dish
with shoulders as tense as a bow.

It drapes like newly laundered sheets
as I slice crescent moons of apple in
then watch your pinch of cinnamon

sprinkle darkly down. And finally, the lid.
Then me, as usual, trying to shape the scraps
into some special smile for each of us.

Admiral FitzRoy's Barometer

I've found a narrow space for it up the stairs
between the photographs of fishing nets
and the lighthouse with pom-pom rocks.

I love the tiny writing on pale blue,
the graduated pen and inks of clouds,
the cherubs' cheeks puffed out
as if trying to blow in my ear
when I walk past.

Above, the Velux window darkens.
Leaves scatter higher than trees.
A house martin chirrups on the line
outcalling all the conversations
backwards and forwards
beneath its feet.

Then splodge and splat,
now faster,
as rain kamikazes on the glass
and the long barometer
(had the tube of mercury
not broken yesterday
when wind slammed the door)
indicates a rising pressure
beyond Admiral FitzRoy's expectation
and silver beads, like perfect moons,
multiply on the landing
so I have been unable to move
for some time now.

Katya

Not of my own choosing
do my paps darken like muzzles.
My belly slowly swells.
I cannot see my valley now.
I crave for lassi
but they bring us rusty water
in the bottom of a can.

They come and come,
day, night, day,
unbuttoning
as the door slaps against the stucco.
They leave our thighs and faces
crusty with their stink.

And after me,
they hump across on to my mother,
covering her shrunken face
with her heavy dirndl skirt.
She is dry, dry.
Her womb is a husk.

Each day I am ripening.
I do not want this cuckoo
fluttering its rabid wings
in my darkness.
I can see its wild eyes beneath my skin.
It will suck me dry as rock.

Yet, I have practised its birth –
how I will keep my legs far apart,
my eyes screwed shut,
then roll it with my heel in the dust
kicking it and its afterbirth
down the mountainside.

Or, how I will say, *Give me my baby,*
and boy or girl, call it Katya.
That was my mother's name.

Visiting Father in the Side Room off the Geriatric Ward and Reading the Notice Above His Sink.

Wet hands thoroughly.
Apply liquid stop.
Rub palm to charm.
Fright palm first over left dorsum.
Then left alarm over fighting force dumb.
Harm to harm, fingers in too haste.
Racks of stingers to opposing swarms,
lingus interlocked.
Rotational rubbing of right thumb
clasped in deft spurt
and vice reverse.
Raw painful shoving back and forwards
with clasped lingers of might hand.
In left spawn and twice measure
and worse.
Rinse and withdraw hands.
Apply one pleasure of alcohol rub
using the midweek prescribed
for 10-15 year olds. Remember
to keep nails abort and unseen.
Don't forget
to apply for reconditioning cream.
Don't forget
to leave your gown and loves in the bin
and to keep the door closed.
Wash hands. Wash hands. Wash hands.

Stone

What accident, what chance
we met? That from a single point
this stone has travelled out
through fire and ice
to find rest here,
cradled in my palm ?

It might have been
a whirlpool eye of Venus,
dust howling across Mars
or part of the firmament
telescopes cannot reach.
A comet's tail writing the sky.

Sh! It stretches in my hand
and yawns. A million eyes open.
What colours! Lashes fine as frost.
I hum a lullaby and one by one
its eyes begin to close.
Has my life been wasted? it dreams.

Was my voice too soft?

Interlude

Some nights I wake to find
I'm back in the cave,
my mother faint with days of heave and push,
not knowing yet,
what her ancient midwife knew,
how, on entering the world,
my dainty cloven hooves pointed to the future.

I'm in that future now,
my hooves more gnarled and notched.
I'm crashing through the woods, or was,
or will be. Something happens there
that links me to mud and fire, sky and ice.
I'm used to the flames in my pelvis,
my glistening red mast –
delicious when they scream and run,
me pounding after,
always having my way in the meadows.

Her next contraction
unveiled my piebald ankles,
then long, strong thighs,
my fur, glittering with birth sac.
You have a boy, the midwife told my mother.
All ram, she did not dare to say,
her eyes as wide as the bowls beside her
covered with sheepskins.
Later she'd need these
to swaddle my goat parts
and present me gorgeous and human
into my mother's pale arms.

So what am I doing here
splashing in the turbid river, smashing lilies
so that their pretty heads swirl away?
Even the dragon-fly has darted
to a cooler, stiller place.
Why am I among these reeds
plucking the loveliest?

I heard the midwife say
that as she delivered my crown
two golden horns erupted among my curls.
She tried to rearrange my hair, conceal them,
but their shadow curves grew,
overwhelmed my mother's bed.

Such a patient reed. I draw its pith,
use my hardened horns to pierce its stem
and fashion pipes, my tongue to moisten them.
Oh sweet, sweet music!
As sweet as my elusive nymph.
But I'll not fail. I will brand her.

When my mother
guided my mouth towards her breast,
I kicked away my fleece in joy:
those blue veins like gentle rivers.
All my love was hers
but she flew out and up the mountainside
howling and keening from its tip.

We've never seen each other since.
And what a favour she did me.
Great Gods
need to stand on their own two feet.
My pipes, this music, merely an interlude.

Seeking a Bittern

Just before dawn they wake me,
so I find myself
pushing through centuries of reeds
into another life.

To find them,
it's black squelching mud
and a meshwork of roots
back from a time when,
as a child, I could have reached out
to touch the passing Moon.

Again! That deep sonic boom,
long speckled throats
close to the swollen river.

Bitterns have never
appeared in my life,
but their sound
bursts through our air
as if we are shipping
caught in their fog.

Fast flowing water
calls as it rises.
It haunts these dark groves
and the broken hearts of the nests
swirling past in the half-light,
nests I almost mistook for eddies.

Again! That deep sonic boom,
long speckled throats
close to the swollen river.
Elusive and urgent, a last few males
call for their mates to locate them

and sooner than silence.

In Praise of the Oologists' Art

You have to admire their patience;
long before night-vision binoculars,
a pin-point focus shaded by two hands.
All that waiting through crepuscular light
as dawn turns leaves blood-red then gold.

A man from Cleethorpes adapted his ladder
by adding a metal crosier head to each rail
so having reached a sturdy lower branch
he could stretch and hook a higher one
then climb again, dittoing upwards. Simply

genius. Of course, he could never patent it
and soon all eggers had their own.
His innovation spread on winged whispers.
And such beautiful primed bodies secreted
under thermal layers and down-filled anoraks.

Hours spent on press-ups, pounding lanes.
How else to clamber and descend a cliff
or scale a crag, inch up a swaying tree-top,
one hand left free? Such dexterity
to lift the clutch into a straw-lined tin.

It takes thirteen years to perfect this art; seven
for 'Recognition' from the house sparrow
to rarity; to learn greenish eggs are from a tree,
the speckled ones, a bush or near the ground;
to drill a tiny hole, cut sacs with a scalpel.

Then the fastidiousness of catalogue, columns,
a quill pen dipped in black to scribe
an A.O.U. Species Number on each shell.
Plus another six more years
to perfect these individual stages.

But the apogee - new osprey eggs
swaddled in cotton wool, arranged
in narrow drawers with a cedar sawdust bed.
This last, the way a midwife lowers a stillborn
into its mother's arms. As expert as that.

Grass

(Surely the people is grass. Is XI 7)

Gather a root of grass
from every lawn in the world,
every sports pitch and gutter,
barrack and hospital ground,
fold yard and pasture, watery bank,
concrete crevice and crack,
wherever grass might force through
to wave its green flags.

And look under things
like wagons shunted away
down the branch line, a churn,
rusting headstocks, long-handled tools,
the soles of the man left waiting.
Yellow it might be
but grass knows how to survive.
It never complicates air.
It travels the world
by linking arms with its neighbour.

With these roots, start a new lawn
in a place where everyone
can walk barefoot across it
(at least once in their lives) to feel
how something as simple as grass
knows how to sing so flutey and free
you need to get down on your knees
and tune your ear to its frequency.
O grass, what have we made you hear?

And after we named you 'grass'
then renamed you 5^1(TTTAGGG) n-3^1,
what words did the wind bring
to make you cower and tremble?

Nimble Will, Squirrel Tail, Tumble and Quitch,
Quaking Grass, Ribbon Grass, Velvet and Witch,
Bristle, Spear, Panic, Redtop and Switch,
why have we made you brandish your swords?

What do you know?

Grasshopper

Each time I am born
it is more burdensome.

The skies are a deeper indigo
and the Moon I loved to leap to
has spun further from me.

All the meadows
where I would unpack my violin,
make them ring with chirp and rasp,
have shrunk. Where is
their deep foam of flowers?

What am I good for
when not even my old wings are needed
to cover the Fairy Midwife's carriage?
How I long for the sound of a child
coming to torment me.

My head is heavy with these things.

Once, I thought nothing of springing
to the bamboo fields round Tokyo,
the bladed pastures of Peru -
there and back in less than a day!
Little Grasshopper,
lutanists across the world would sing,
*Little Grasshopper, shelter from the mid-day sun
in the scarecrow's sleeve.* But everyday now,
a thick wind bangs another door.

Soon the whole world will be without song,
the hollow-jointed stems of grass
become Earth's mute hair.

Forecast

for my father

I'd not have known you in your dimming light,
the way that shadows shrunk your breath
until it slipped its mooring with you in tow.

They said those last few days
had pared you down – as fast
as tapering a candle to fit the candlestick.

You disappeared into the night
just ten minutes
before your wall clock chimed the hour.

My radio, a hundred miles away,
prepared to circumnavigate
Low Faroes, Viking, FitzRoy.

Then, *A Vigorous Low, Severe Gale 9,*
Violent Storm 11. Somehow I knew
not to call the coastguard.

A corona of automatic beams
sweep round from the land's vague edge.
Somewhere, a candle guttering.

That completes the Shipping Forecast
a voice says, before, *Wishing you*
a very good night. And then the pips.

The First Moose To Try It

Although the lichen here is plentiful
and exactly the same shade of green
as in the next pastureland, surely
there's more to being Moose than this?

There's something I've been dreaming of
for generations. I've not discussed it
but have seen in pools and lakes how birds
diverge from sighing treetops into free.

A mountain peak near Vatnestrom.
A moon with both eyes wide open.
Then stepping off, starssuddentwinkling
andtinklingchandeliers as they fly past.

Rushing wind sings in my horns,
my silky beard streams like a comet's tail,
my frost-tipped hooves pedal through air.
I'm as light as a snowflake.

And I would have kept on going,
perhaps with a swerve up to Pegasus,
to be near his wise, my family looking up
might have seen Constellation Moose,

if it hadn't been for that yellow car
with double-barrelled guns pointing
through windows at the moon behind me
and two men in moose-fur flap hats, their

one-eyed inane grins closing on me fast.
Back there among the lakes and lichen
there was every reason not to leave
and every different reason why I should.

The Old Observatory

after reading Montale

You may or may not recall
how half its brick staircase had collapsed
so we had to improvise with ropes
to reach the viewing floor.

The scope pillar was still there
and we could see the raw edge
where they'd used oxy-acetylene
to cut the precision mount free.

You pushed the dome round with one hand
then found the brass chase and ratchet
to open its narrow slit, setting free
a stellar flash of butterflies.

Then, from nowhere, hailstones clattered down
the size of planets, or so you said,
as you unhooked me and we became
as breathless as those first astronomers here

who also must have thought
they'd brought the Universe into focus.
Passing overhead in tonight's bright dark
the space station burns a hungry hole

and the stars that once were ours
(because that evening we named each one)
are blurred. You could be anywhere. How long
can you remain while never having stayed?

Feeding the Bi-valve

Somewhere overhead
your plane is heading out.
So many thousand feet,
so many miles per hour,
so many gallons of fuel to burn.
The noughts are meaningless.
I only know that I could string them
like a double row of pearls
and they'd weigh heavy
round my neck.

Even though it fills the sky
I'll not look up. I'll not look up again
while it flies away from me.
Besides, more importantly,
the tank needs cleaning out
and there's all the watery mouths to feed.
O-O-O, they pout, O-O-O,
sending tiny pearl bubbles
to pop at the surface,
momentarily disturb its skin.

Fish glint past oblivious
swimming their own unclear sky.
They know no time, only same-same-same.
Sometimes food drifts down
from somewhere. Here in this corner
the bi-valve has opened
exposing its simple hunger.
A single translucent limb points upward
until I rap on the glass, watch it recoil
into its barnacle-encrusted shell.

The Widower's Button

I asked you for thread and needle
to repair our sudden heat
but her straw sewing basket
(pink raffia flowers, a butterfly)
contained all your married years:
the children's woven name tapes,
her suture scissors, the repair kit
from a hotel in Beijing.
Odd buttons and press studs
fastening the four of you together.

She must have used this same needle,
this same white thread,
easing them along cotton hems,
newly laundered shirts,
the smell of sheets fresh from the line.

I was to have sewn your white button on,
but instead I am threading gaps
into a patchwork
whose pattern I can only glimpse
through photographs and ornaments,
the bathroom shelf,
what I imagine behind those wardrobe doors.

I take up her embroidery:
a perfect lawn in variegated strands,
feather stitch and satin stitch,
lazy daisies along an unfinished path.
It's left with the threaded needle in
as if the phone had rung
or she'd gone to put the kettle on.

You bring me a cup of tea,
watch me flounder with the button.
The needle's point
refuses to come up through the hole.
The cotton twists back on itself,
ends up in knots
I have to tease out gently,
knowing that if I try too hard
I might slip and prick my finger,
snap the thread.

In The Consulting Room

Do sit down, he says,
pointing to the jolly-coloured chair
perhaps assuming
they'll sit on each other's knees.
He picks up the phone,
requests another be brought in.

They're joined at the sternum,
have shared the same blouses
and stretchy cardigans, heart,
for twenty years.
Their memories and imaginations
have been visited by the same blood. At night,
they pass the same breath between them.
It wreathes their dreams.
Sometimes, their lips rest on each other's.

*So how have you been? Any problems
since I last saw you?*

nono, they reply,
pulling at their knitted cuffs.

Stairs still manageable? Sleep well?

yesyes

Eating? Any difficulty there? Bowels?

nono

They reach for a mint
from each other's pocket.

A clinical sister brings in an x-ray,
fixes it against the light box.
And leaves.
They both turn their heads,
see a pattern of pale bones
like snowy branches,
timber from a ghost ship.
They see a huge dark shape
hung from the spars,
a pulsar, an exploding star.

So, have you thought about
what we talked about last time,
reached a decision?

Sweet wrappers spill from their laps.

yesyes. nono. yesno.

In Praise of Grey

Of all colours
grey paints the wisest.
It tiptoes along the rosary
to illuminate uncertainties.
Its muscley arms brace apart
basalt and marble pillars.
It can upturn chiaroscuro's hat
brimful with expectation.
Shadows try and hide in it
and fail, grey's finger
pointing to the temporary
moon and sun.
Grey patrols the edges and folds
between oil and salt,
between falling snow
and fallout's blot.
In the kiln
it sits astride the pyrometer
soaked equally by
the white heat of porcelain
and cold, dark shelves.
It links albatross and water boatman,
panther and cabbage white.
Grey, our ganglions and brain cells.
It is fired with endless desire
for all things to be possible.
And this, in lakefuls,
I leave to you my son,
and for you, his sister,
knowing how
a silver paddle
to keep it stirred and fresh.

Wholly

I'm following my feet to Midnight Mass
between gravestones and halogen lamps
tilted to bathe the spire in amber —
long histories reaching through darkness.

A haloed moon lights the path
unvisited since routine years
but it's the same flickering row of pews,
the organ's umbral sub-bass and diapason.

Curious how I still bow my head and kneel,
mirror the rest of the congregation
but when the vicar speaks of light and dark,
how they lean against each other,

there's something shines out
from between his consonants and vowels
bright enough to illuminate us all.
As he raises the silver chalice, breaks bread,

I find myself in a shuffle-forward with the rest
wishing I could fill my pockets with hosts
for those outside these walls: wild animals,
livestock, creatures that move along the earth.

I'd hold no guilt if bottles clanked in my coat.
Seed-bearing plants and fruiting trees,
fluttering things, others that teem in water —
should only those at the altar rail receive?

Tonight, this stony place magnifies
the eloquence of both night and day.
Pray not a crumb or drop be wasted.
Truly, verily, surely. May shadows pass.

The Wash

Father, forgive us for finding you out this way,
your three children undressing you
to look like Mammy's plucked goose lying there.
    How you'd hate us to see this naked truth
preferring your weather-hardened coat
buttoned to the chin, your tight-laced boots,
                              your pulled-down cap.
We are charged with the task of bathing you
before the delicacy of your shroud,
your skin suddenly our own skin.
    We are amazed to find we even share
the same imperfections of our feet —
toes three and four like Siamese twins.
I'm soaping them while Michael wipes
what he says is a tear from your eye.
    You always told us that to cry
was a breached dam or broken fence
the herd could wander through.
                              And when Colm
shook out your pockets just now
instead of knives and baler twine,
there were sacks of seed.
    And was that a lake,
a full sun swimming in it?
    Your crumpled handkerchief
contained a shower of moths and butterflies
enough to fan the whole Earth
into a different orbit, or further.
                              And then Father,
from deeper in your pocket,
a nest enclosing three warm and freckled eggs.

A Very Private Conversation

Surrounded by a summer sea of sky
and as many shades of green
as years of history,
I am content
to lie back on this fringed scarp
and speak to a god.

I tell him that here,
in the crooked arm of the valley,
quiet with grasshoppers and curlew,
the trattle of quaking grass,
I'm unafraid of the past
weighted with death,
unafraid of dying here,
how I hope the crows

will profit from my flesh
and leave my bones
gleaming in chalk and flint;
that I could invite death
to come now
but how
I will not write this poem
until tomorrow.